Tasteless Cup of Tea

Odyssey of dreams pursued and destinies revealed.

ROBIN GEORGE

This book is specially meant for the young readers of the world around.

Contents

Preface

Growing up today can feel like an exciting but confusing journey. With so many choices and changes, it is easy to feel lost or unsure.

This book is here to help you find your way. In this book, you will find simple advice and stories that can guide you through the ups and downs of being young. It is written to help you understand yourself better, make good choices and feel more confident about your future.

Each chapter shares ideas and tips to help you handle challenges, build your skills and stay true to who you are. You will learn how to face changes bravely, think creatively and make decisions that fit your own dreams and goals.

As you read, I hope this book becomes your friend and guide, helping you to discover your strengths and shape a future that is right for you. Welcome to a journey of finding yourself.

Robin George

06 – 06 – 2024

Acknowledgments

I dedicate this book to those who have enriched my thoughts in my journey and to one person who has been the greatest source of inspiration for me. This book is especially for them.

I appreciate the exceptional people in my life, especially my students who have shaped my ideas.

I am deeply grateful to Mr. Karunakaran Perambra, Ms. Aiswarya Kuriakose and Helna Catharine Jaison for their editorial assistance, Mr. Binu K.K. for the illustrations and Mr. Supreeth N. B. for designing the cover page. Their valuable contributions have made this work possible.

Prologue

As I sat on the sofa, watching the fleeting lives of the Robin birds outside and listening to their sweet chirping, I felt the urge for a cup of tea.

I called out to my sister, who was busy making delicious pudding in the kitchen, and asked her to bring me a cup.

She questioned me, "Hey! Haven't you had anything to drink already?"

"Yes," I replied, "but I'd like another cup of tea. Can I have one?"

She sighed and replied gently, "Of course."

Soon, my sister returned with a cup of tea, her expression serious.

After taking a sip, I realized it was unsweetened and bland. My sister scolded me, warning about the dangers of diabetes.

But I reassured her, saying I could handle it.

She added two teaspoons of sugar and I stirred slowly.

As I took my first sip, something caught my eye, causing me to recline on the sofa.

I heard the clock ticking, signaling it was five in the evening. The gentle drizzle outside and the soft breeze caressing my face whispered for me to close my eyes. And so, I did.

It was truly a moment of tranquility, the finest day in my life.

1. Polish Your Shoes

"Action is the foundational key to all success."

- Pablo Picasso

Once, a friend told me about a place where neglecting to polish your shoes could have serious consequences. The receptionist's main task was to find those who come improperly dressed. After hearing this, I decided to always take the time to polish my shoes.

We often spend time making our faces presentable, but hardly anyone thinks about polishing their shoes. Why? It's a simple question. Those who strive for perfection start with their shoes. It doesn't take long, but it makes a difference.

I remember a small incident involving Unnikkuttan, a diligent 5th grader. One day, his friends were shocked by his unusual behavior—he shouted at a friend for stepping on his polished shoes. That morning, his mother had to struggle to wake him up. He remembered his teacher's command: anyone without polished shoes would face the scorching sun and the principal's office.

In a panic, he sought his mother's help. She didn't understand his urgency, so he took matters into his own hands. He scrubbed and polished his shoes until they shone. For the first time, he could see his reflection in them.

Proud and confident, he boarded the bus, feeling like a hero. His classmates noticed and complimented him. It was an unforgettable moment—he realized that small efforts can bring great attention. For the first time, he felt truly special.

Unnikkuttan carefully stepped off the bus, checking his polished shoes more than ten times before entering his classroom, V-A. As the teacher inspected everyone's shoes, she was amazed by the shine on Unnikkuttan's shoes and praised him. That day, he felt incredibly proud.

Motivation plays a crucial role in shaping our lives. Yet, many people hesitate to acknowledge others' achievements, whether out of insecurity or fear of losing their own status. This reluctance to appreciate others stems from a deep-seated ego.

Rabindranath Tagore once said, "You should keep your head high," but sometimes pride distorts this message. If children aren't praised for good deeds, they might grow up without knowing how to appreciate others. If they don't experience it, they won't know how to give it.

For instance, if a school principal doesn't praise a top student because he couldn't achieve success, it's a missed opportunity for encouragement. Francis of Assisi wisely stated,

"Power and position make us forget our true nature."

Thankfully, Unnikkuttan's teacher appreciated him, and he basked in the recognition. Appreciation, however, can be complex. Misunderstandings can arise, turning a positive gesture into a burden.

One day, another boy accidentally stepped on Unnikkuttan's shoe, sparking a conflict. Both were taken to the headmaster, and the teacher who encouraged shoe polishing faced consequences. She has aimed to uplift her students but ended up punished, reflecting the harsh reality that good intentions can sometimes lead to unexpected outcomes.

Life is full of challenges and lessons. Like bees, which tirelessly create the best honey, we should strive to prepare ourselves well. Honey's quality attracts others, and similarly, a well-prepared person draws admiration. Reflect on your life: is it rich and fulfilling? Patience and perseverance are essential like polishing shoes requires time and effort.

"Nothing is more dangerous than an idea when it is the only one you have," said Emile

Chartier. People often overlook the importance of the small things, like shoes, which silently support us. What if they refuse to accompany us due to negligence? Thankfully, they don't.

In essence, take the time to care for the little things in life. They carry us further than we realize.

I feel that people are often too busy to pause and appreciate the small things, like the shoes they wear. No one notices their condition or cleanliness. Someone once said we should thank our shoes for carrying us everywhere without complaint. They simply obey, without argument.

Imagine if one day your shoes could speak and refused to go with you, saying, "I don't want to come because you never wash your feet or clean me." Thankfully, shoes don't have life.

Do you find this thought tasteless?

2. Make a Question against God

"The most common way people give up their power is by thinking they don't have any."

There are times in life when we feel like we are nothing. In those moments, we might call out to God or question Him, asking, "Why did you give me this life?" Some people think that God doesn't see their troubles or that He ignores their pain. When they experience deep suffering for the first time, they ask questions that seem impossible to answer.

One of my professors, a priest who was a friend of Pope Benedict XVI, once shared a real story during a sermon. He spoke about a little girl, around six or seven years old, from a remote village in Jharkhand. His friend saw her carrying a load of firewood on her head while her baby brother was swaddled on her back. She worked so diligently, arranging the firewood perfectly without complaining.

At first, his friend didn't understand what she was doing. She watched her for a while, then approached and asked, "Is it a burden for you, dear girl?"

What a question! If someone asked you this, what would you say? You might think, "Can't you see?" or "Are you blind?" But the girl just looked at her and kept working. She asked her again, but she still didn't answer.

For the third time, she asked the question, but this time with a gentle tone. The girl slowly looked up at her, and their eyes met. She described her gaze as unforgettable, the most piercing and remarkable she had ever seen. It felt like her eyes were trying to convey something important.

She finally spoke, "How can it be a burden? It's not a burden; it's my brother."

For a moment, they both stood in silence with tears in their eyes. It was a powerful reflection—nobody could have expected such a response. To this child, what seemed like a burden was actually a blessing, a presence of God.

This story reveals two important ideas: first, the child was fulfilling her parents' duty, and second, she willingly took on the responsibility herself.

In some places, it's common for women to carry their babies on their backs while they work. It's a normal part of their daily life. So, when a 6-year-old girl takes on the responsibility of caring for her younger sibling without complaint while her parents are away, it's truly remarkable.

This girl challenges us all with her silent question: "Do you truly have faith in God? Why do you curse Him during your hardships, the same God who gave you life?"

Can we answer these questions? If we can respond like this child, perhaps we can see burdens as blessings. Let's all pray for such strength and faith.

Many people don't want to be patient or face difficulties. We believe that God has a plan for us, but when good things disappear, how do we continue to praise Him?

"The quality of our expectations determines the quality of our action."

- Andre Godin

Religious texts like the *Quran*, the *Bhagavad Gita* and the *Bible* teach that humans are God's best creation. If we are made in His image, the person next to us also reflects God, though we often forget this. As Sreenarayana Guru said, "Aham Brahmasmi" which means if the presence of God is there in you means you are really God. If God is within us, we must reflect on our character and actions.

Sadly, people often use harsh words and actions against their own family and neighbors. Scriptures predict times of conflict within families and nations. Scripture speaks that there will be a time when son will turn against the father, daughter against mother, son-in-law against father-in-law, daughter-in-law against mother-in-law nation against nation, etc. If we are truly God's finest creation, then He has a plan for us. How can He abandon us? No loving father would give a snake when his child asks for bread.

It's our duty to discover God's plan for our lives. If we fail to do so, it's our own fault. We may be rich or poor, Muslim, Hindu or Christian but when we die, we should be remembered as good humans. Blaming God for our shortcomings is not fair. He created us. Is it His mistake? I don't think so.

I was deeply moved by a story about Alexander the Great. Before he died, he asked his hands to be left outside his coffin to show, despite his greatness, that he left this world with nothing. This story always inspires me and reminds me to speak about it whenever I can.

We might face many failures in life, but even in death, our shadow stays with us, showing our journey. Before that it might have gone through many places, travelled with us to wherever we have travelled, but now at the end it lies with us. In our final moments, we might curse God for our mistakes, but blaming our Creator is unjust.

Do you think it is tasteless?

3. Talent Is Yours, You Choose

"We have to do the best we can. This is our sacred human responsibility."

Everyone is gifted with unique talents, but not everyone realizes what theirs' are. Many people chase big dreams without understanding their true strengths. As Becket said, "Everyone goes with bigger tides only with lower ones we can identify how many naked ones are there."

Some people are rebels and hide their talents, while others, even without much talent, get attention because of their background. It's common to see doctors' children becoming doctors and engineers' children becoming engineers. Because parents worry about their children's futures; they buy ranks and positions with the aid of money. But how many parents of privileged backgrounds help talented children of poor farmers? Even talented children are rejected due to the cunningness of these kinds of people who is wealthy to purchase anything.

True talent needs to be recognized and nurtured. I know there are people with multi-talents. They can perform almost all activities in a better manner. But do we appreciate those people? Or do they come forward by themselves? Obviously not, they are worried about something, may be the society, or their own life's existence. Some people have many talents but fear society's judgment or worry about their own survival. Even in schools, some of the teachers skip their work by attributing the idea on the head of some students. These students are acting teachers and real teachers are passive listeners.

How do we develop our talents? No one will come and tell you what your talents are; you have to discover them yourself. We await another opportunity to come without knowing opportunity waits for none. When the door of opportunity shuts, it shuts forever."People may see the joker as a joker, but he sees himself as a performer."

Charlie Chaplin, in his autobiography, shared that he once asked a soothsayer about his future. The soothsayer told him he had a bright future, not as a dramatist, but in a similar role. Chaplin made the world laugh. If he hadn't focused on his talent, someone else might have taken his place.

A small lizard can climb the terrace of a king's palace. We must be wise like a snake and humble like a dove. We can only judge our future from what we have suffered in the past. Right now we must choose to withstand with anything that comes to our life. You need always a reason to fight and to achieve success in your life.

"The secret of getting ahead is getting started." The journey of a thousand miles begins with a single step, even if we don't know where it will lead. Therefore I always appreciate the one who has the vigor of starting.

J.K. Rowling, the author of Harry Potter, wanted to be a writer. At six, she wrote her first story. She faced rejection from twelve publishers but kept going because her sister encouraged her. In 1997, she succeeded, and now her books are loved worldwide.

Overthinking can stop us from acting. Instead, we should start and see what happens. How many of us count the steps when we climb the steps? Most of us don't count the steps we take;

we just move forward. A child doesn't know his future but follows the path in front of him.

Nobody knows what we will become or where life will take us. We often reach our destination without much effort, but it may not be what we wanted.

A child may dream of being a great performer and plan for it, but until he actually performs on stage, he cannot truly call himself a performer.

For example, there was a young girl who decided to participate in an interschool fest hosted by a national school. She practiced classical dance every day with her teacher for three hours, perfecting different mudras. She believed in herself and was confident she would win. She eagerly waited for the day to come.

But what can we do? Everything is part of God's plan. What happened to her? Did she perform?

Sadly, she met with an accident and was hospitalized. Her awaited chance was lost. How did it happen? What would you do in such a situation? We often start cursing our destiny.

Remember, the moment is always yours. Every moment of your performance is important. Until you are on stage performing, no one will recognize your talent or call you great.

To be honest, you become a master only after completing your task. Then, people will say good things about you. Only then you can proudly say that you have achieved your goal.

That moment will be yours, and you will shine like the sun among the stars.

We often sit in the classroom and daydream, but how many of those dreams come true? To achieve your dreams, you need to start taking action now.

Zig Ziglar once said, "You don't have to be great to start, but you have to start to be great."

Does it feel tasteless to you?

4. We Are the Creator of Our Own Destiny

"All powers are within you, you can do anything and everything."

- Swami Vivekananda

Even the great Vararuji couldn't determine his destiny. He ended up marrying a girl from a lower caste whom he once tried to harm. The question that puzzled him was the same: "Does everything depend upon our destiny?"

What can we do if our destiny goes against our wishes? Most of the time, it does.

Do you think it's because God knows what we need, or is it our own greed? We often desire for everything we can afford, and if we don't get it, we might blame our parents.

Let me share the story a friend told me about his life. He was an excellent student, eagerly waiting for his SSLC Board exam results. When the newspaper arrived, he ran five kilometers to get it. After seeing his marks, he spent Rs 1.50/-to buy it. He ran home with such joy that he could have won a medal at the Olympics. When he told me this, he laughed, a wild laugh.

He arrived home to find his father sitting in the parlor, tightening the spade.

"Papa! The results are out. I passed with distinction. Look at my marks," he said with a sigh.

His father simply looked at him, smiled and went back to his work.

He waited patiently for his father to say something, but as his father continued working without acknowledging him, he made some noise and waited for the attention of his father.

The most joyous moment for any child is sharing their exam results with their parents, hoping for celebration together. But what if that doesn't happen? I leave it to the readers to ponder and find an answer.

"Can I choose science, Papa? I want to study. Can I join plus one?" His father paused his work, lifted his head, and looked at the boy.

"My son, you're bright, but you know our financial situation. I can't afford a scientific calculator, so I suggest humanities if you wish to continue your studies."

It's a challenging situation for any father to deny his bright son's aspirations, but circumstances can be tough. The father had no other option. Eager to study, the boy took a job as a bus cleaner to earn money.

He worked hard for two months until he met a bus driver, who unexpectedly became his guiding light. He inquired about his marks, and upon hearing them, the man shouted, "From tomorrow, don't come here. This isn't where you belong. Pursue your studies, aim for greatness. Get into school, focus on humanities." The phrase 'humanities, humanities' echoed in his ears.

With no choice, he left and enrolled in grade twelve, feeling elated.

In everyone's life, there are moments that change everything. Now, he's a genuine person, holding degrees and successful positions in business. If he hadn't worked hard and listened to the advice of the driver, he might have just been a good driver. But time transformed him into not just a good driver, but also a successful entrepreneur. He didn't achieve success by idling in comfort; he worked hard and put his heart into it. He excelled in his studies, earning top grades in high school, college and post-graduation. You only meet someone who completely changes your life once in a lifetime.

Sometimes, you meet someone who changes everything for you. You can share your deepest thoughts, dreams, and fears with them. When something amazing happens, they're the first person you want to tell, and they always support you. You can be yourself around them without worrying about judgment. Destiny isn't something we choose; it's something that happens by chance. When life gets tough, we might blame destiny, but making the right choices can shape our lives. Life is about making choices to create beauty and meaning.

I recommend making your own choices. No one will tell you exactly what to focus on. Think about a white shirt. It's just white, but the brand can make it more expensive or popular. We choose certain brands because we trust them or know about them. Even though the color is the same, we still pick a specific brand. Why? It is because we have options. Without brands, everyone might choose the same thing. Brands give products value and status. For example, if a teacher wears branded clothes, students might think highly of them and show them more respect. Brands can influence how people perceive others.

Now, branding has become popular in Kerala too. Woodland shoes were originally made for people working in tar and excavation areas. The company created sturdy shoes to help those in difficult jobs. But now, we consider them perfect for everyday wear. Look at how things have changed in our area.

Throughout our lives, we make choices. Do you think all your choices are right? No, they're not always right. But we still accept them because we have no other option. Life is ours to live. So, don't worry about your choices. Trust that the ones you make are the best for you. Start making the right choices and believe they are the best. Become the creator of your own destiny.

"God does not want us to succeed, He only asks us to try"

Let me ask you a simple question: How many experts do you think are born with natural talents? Everyone has to work hard to achieve their goals. Do you think it's easy for someone who just sits in a comfortable room?

Experts are not born; they are made through consistent practice. Practice is the key to achieving perfection. It helps us overcome life's challenges. Hard work is like medicine that brings miracles in life.

Not everyone experiences the power of hard work equally, but there's always a chance to find your rhythm in life. Let's unlock the power of practice together.

Do you find this tasteless?

5. Find the Meaning of Your Life

"If you can't do great things, do small things in a great way"

- Napoleon Hill

We are all created in God's image, so we should be able to find the meaning of our lives. Our lives are like a rose, calling for notice. When people come across it, they stop to admire its beauty and smell its lovely scent.

What led us to this point? Once, in my life, there was a little girl who always enjoyed walking with me. Whenever we walked, she held my hand and never wanted me to carry her. She shared her beautiful stories and life experiences with me. This made me very happy because she was sharing her secrets. One day something happened that made me think deeply. We were tired from walking, so we decided to go inside and have some coffee. I went to the kitchen and made two cups of coffee. Before that, I had her sit on a chair. We both sat there and enjoyed our coffee.

She stretched out her arms, and I picked her up and placed her on the table. After finishing our coffee, she stood on the table and asked me to put her down. Standing beside the table, I wanted to test her, so I stretched out my arms and told her to jump. She looked at me.

I encouraged her again to jump; she listened and jumped towards me. I assured her I would catch her, and there was nothing to worry about.

I can't fully express how it felt when she listened to me. What made her do that? Why did she jump? She trusted herself and knew I wouldn't let her fall; I would catch her and keep her safe. It was her trust in me. I'm sure she believed in me. If you ever feel like you're falling and can't get up, remember that God's power will be there to lift you up.

"I held the trunk with both my hands

And looked abroad in foreign lands"

Imagine that in your growth, many people have helped and played a crucial role. When you sit high up on a large tree, you may not think about anyone.

When you achieve everything in your life, if you forget the people who helped you, remember they are like the trunk that supports you on the tree. Don't forget the past, because if you do, you might forget the important moments that contributed to your growth and the people who planted the seeds of your success.

Now you are skilled at walking. But if your parents hadn't helped you when you were learning, do you think you'd be so good at it now? You can walk, run and fall, but you should know how to get back up.

How many of you have thanked your mother and father for this? Probably none. When you fall, what's the first thing you do? You look around to see if anyone saw you. If someone did, you feel embarrassed. If no one did, you feel relieved and move on.

But remember, the first time you fell, you learned how to get up and build your self-esteem. Falling down is not a great failure. I assure you, it's the start of becoming stronger and learning to stand on your own.

"Life is not meant to be easy, my child; but take courage, it can be delightful."

What is the meaning of your life? How many of you have asked yourself this question? And how many have found an answer?

Siddhartha had to leave his palace to find the answer. Did he succeed? He became a great man who transformed the world, but he had to give up all life's pleasures.

How many of you are willing to give up life's pleasures? Everyone seeks pleasure, but no one is truly satisfied.

I asked some students a simple question: if you see a rose, what would you do? Out of 30 students, 25 said they would pluck the flower. The rose offers its life for many to enjoy, yet people want to keep it for themselves. This is a common attitude.

Selfishness is part of our lives and hard to discard. We love to possess whatever we can. We might think we understand the meaning of life, but the question remains unanswered.

We are too focused on our status in society, forgetting to find our true purpose and meaning in life.

Once, I had the chance to ask a simple question to some students: "Who is the president of India?" The answers I received gave me new insights into politics. After hearing all the responses, I asked them, "What do you mean by president?"

I received many answers, but one girl's response made everyone laugh. Are you curious about what she said? She told me, "The president is the second prime minister of India."

The students were stunned by her answer. From her perspective, it made sense. The Indian president isn't as prominent in her eyes; she has only seen posters of the prime minister, not the president. So, she concluded this on her own.

Why did Eve listen to Satan and disobey God? For self-satisfaction. God told them not to eat the fruit from the tree in the middle of paradise. But Eve listened to Satan, disobeyed God, and shared the fruit with her husband Adam, who also ate it. Adam listened to his wife. What was behind their actions? Selfishness. We should remember we are the descendants of Adam and Eve.

Adam had to toil the ground due to the curse, and this curse continues even today. Many people have found the meaning of their lives. Why can't you be one of them? I'm not saying you should become like Eve or Adam, but become your true self and find your life's meaning.

It might be a difficult task, but everything is in your hands. You are the creator of your destiny. Your destiny begins and ends with you. So, always ask yourself, "Why am I on this earth? Is there something God wants me to do?" Try to find out, and you will succeed.

Does this sound tasteless?

6. I Am Who I Am

"There is no charm equal to tenderness of heart."

- Jane Austin

"The remarkable entry or reentry to your life is to remark yourself." What does this mean? Do we take time to listen to our friends? Some share everything, while others keep things to themselves. How many of us take time to listen to our friends' problems and try to help? Or do we just share our own problems, dismissing theirs?

Listening is one of the greatest virtues. As God said, "One, who has ears to listen, let him listen."

Once, during a night class, a boy asked if he could go to the toilet. You might think this is trivial, but sometimes small events have great significance. So, I allowed him to go.

The funny part is that after reaching the toilet, he began to cry loudly. Everyone could hear him. Worried, I ran to the toilet, thinking he might have fallen. Some students followed, curious about what had happened. Fortunately, nothing was wrong.

I asked him, "What happened?" He continued crying as if he had a stomachache. But his answer made everyone laugh.

The next day was his birthday, and he had called his father to take him out of the hostel to buy chocolates for his friends and teachers. His father arrived at 4:30 pm, and when the boy saw him, he ran and hugged him, saying, "I think you love me."

It was a joyful moment for the child, meeting his father after a long time in the hostel. They went out, had a nice meal at a 3-star hotel, and the boy ate to his heart's content.

But now, back at the hostel, he was crying in the toilet. I asked him why he was unhappy. He explained that he had eaten so much delicious food, but now it was all going to waste as he had to use the toilet. He felt it was a waste of such a wonderful experience and worried he wouldn't get another chance like that soon.

The children around us and I couldn't help but laugh at his innocent concern. He continued, saying he had enjoyed the food so much, but now it felt pointless because he couldn't keep it forever. Sitting beside his father and eating whatever he wanted was a rare joy for him, and he was sad it was over.

I had no words to console him. The pain of a child is unique to him. Who can truly understand it? Pleasure and pain are personal experiences; others can only observe. We might say we are like drops of water in the ocean.

His answer left everyone stunned, and you can guess what happened next. If such an incident occurred in your life, how would you handle it?

He wasn't crying from a stomachache, needing the toilet at an inconvenient time, or from an injury. So why was he crying?

It was the pain of nostalgia. He had enjoyed his favourite varieties of food, and now he knew it would be another year before he could celebrate his birthday again. The feelings of joy from eating with his father made him cry.

How many of you cry when you throw away food your mother prepared? Most of us discard food and move on, making our lives comfortable.

Whenever we have a chance to perform, we love to do it in front of an audience. If we get the best spot, especially center stage, we are thrilled.

"It is in the treatment of trifles that a person shows what they are."

- Arthur Schopenhauer

Imagine a time when people eagerly take on tasks they don't know how to perform well. They might not be the best at it; they cause issues, disrupting the teacher's efforts. What a situation when you are indulged like this. Often, it's not just the children but their parents who are fighting to show their worth.

In a dance performance, the best performer should be at the center. But sometimes, you see the best dancer in a corner because he or she is the child of a poor peasant. If the selection committee picks the right person, the child who wanted to be in the center might cry at home to get their parents' attention. The parents then pressure the selectors: "If my child isn't given the main spot, they will quit the dance." To keep the peace or perhaps for other motives, the committee chooses the recommended child, even if they aren't the best performer.

Who is truly responsible for selecting the right person? Is it the judge or those who influence the judge?

Life has its share of agony and despair, but remember you are filled with great potential. When God created you, He instilled love, wisdom, imagination and ideas in you. Yet, we often feel dissatisfied with what we have. Bill Gates said,

"It's not your fault if you are born poor, but it's your fault if you die poor."

Sometimes, you are told you are great, and other times your great deeds go unnoticed. How can they appreciate you if they don't recognize your efforts? You might have dreams of greatness and decide to make changes, but obstacles hold you back.

True understanding comes from the heart. Only those who have been appreciated can truly appreciate others. How can we cultivate appreciation? Why do we appreciate others? What do we gain from it? Do we lose anything by appreciating others? These questions might seem insignificant, but they touch on fundamental human feelings.

Similarly, if you have experienced real pain, how do you share that knowledge? Those who have faced traumatic situations can understand others' pain and offer solace. They can become channels of comfort.

Life has two dimensions. If you focus your heart, you can find treasures within. Do you have a wound? Who will heal it? Do you face challenges? Who will solve them? Do you feel despair? Who will console you? The answer is you. Only you can do these things perfectly.

Who can make a difference? Only you. People accumulate things without knowing when they will leave this world. Still, they collect. Can anyone control their lifespan? No, only destiny can.

Pope Francis said, "Man accumulates everything without knowing when he will go from this land. When he goes, he can take nothing because the coffin has no pockets."

Even if I try 1,000 times to understand my mind, I doubt I will find the answer. How can you climb again when you're at the peak of the mountain? Everyone wants to climb the big mountain despite the barriers. Only faith leads them.

I believe there are two kinds of people: those who truly climbed and reached the top and those who were carried up.

I ask you, if challenges don't teach you a lesson, what will? Each challenge in our life teaches us a valuable lesson, one that cannot be forgotten.

If I can present my life like the stars in the sky, what would that life be like?

Does this seem tasteless to you?

7. We Are All Travellers

"Even the greatest was once a beginner. Don't be afraid to take that first step"

A person who wants to gain something often has to give up something important. Do you agree with this idea? Reflect on these questions:

- How do you feel when you want to be rich?
- How do you feel when you want recognition?
- How do you feel when you want to win?
- How do you feel when you fail?
- How do you feel when you lose loved ones?
- How do you feel when you face problems in life?

Do you think you need to let go of something you value? The experiences teach us to change our old ways. Are humans meant only to face hurt and challenges? No, they should learn from them and be ready to bear life's burdens.

Let's bury or crucify our old selves. Don't always choose the easy path; sometimes choose the difficult one. Why? Because unexpected diamonds may lie there.

"A journey of a thousand miles begins with a single step."

We are all travelers in life. Think of a train: it starts somewhere and ends somewhere else. Sometimes it speeds up, sometimes it slows down and sometimes everything runs smoothly. So is life. We start somewhere and end up somewhere else.

Some passengers board a train without knowing its destination and worry about where they are headed. Some people live their lives like a goods train, carrying everything, even what isn't their responsibility. They don't know what they are doing or the purpose of their life. They live like frogs in a well.

"Most people don't discover how to live until it's time to die – and that's a shame. Most people spend the best years of their lives watching television in a subdivision. Most people die at twenty and buried at eighty."

- Robin Sharma- Discover your destiny.

From the moment a child is born, you might wonder how they perceive the world around them. Who pays attention to such things? Yet, it's true, and I want to share an event that occurred.

The grandfather finds joy in watching wrestling. Whenever he wants, he turns on the TV. While the parents work, the child stays with his grandfather. The child too enjoys watching wrestling and he eagerly waits for the program to begin. Despite advice from others to stop watching it in front of the child, the grandfather ignores them all.

Now, the child is three years old, and the grandfather is hospitalized in ICU. Everyone rushes to the hospital, confused about what happened. Even the child's parents leave their work to go to the hospital.

The reason for this sudden emergency becomes clear when the grandmother, wiping tears from her eyes, speaks up. She was in the kitchen preparing fish curry for lunch when she put the child to sleep in the cradle. However, he didn't sleep. Instead, he sneaked out and watched cartoons. The grandmother scolded him and put him back to sleep, but he murmured something in protest before lying down.

The grandfather, unaware of the scolding the child received earlier, he turned on the TV to watch wrestling. The three-year-old became angry, got up quietly, retrieved a hammer from under the cupboard and approached the grandfather. With two swift blows, he knocked the eighty-kilogram man into a coma.

Eventually, the grandmother rushed into the room upon hearing loud noises. She was perplexed to find her husband lying on the floor while her grandson remained in the cradle, seemingly undisturbed. Despite her efforts to awaken her husband, there was no response. Overwhelmed, she felt faint, but managed to summon a neighbor for help. Now, they were all in the hospital.

What were the consequences of this seemingly small incident? You might find it simple, but if it had truly happened...

The grandfather stopped watching wrestling. He no longer paid heed to others' advice; instead, he learned from his own experiences. Seeing the genuine smile on the child's face warmed his heart.

It might bring a laugh to you as you read it, but think deeply; if it had occurred...

We often act without considering the consequences, paying little heed to the impact of our actions. We encounter both curses and blessings from others. Some see us as a burden, while others find us a source of inspiration, leading to changes in their lives.

There are those who, like Bollywood actor Aamir Khan's character in "3 Idiots," believe that everything is fine regardless of their actions. But what a pity it is!

Sometimes, what seems bad now may have once touched our hearts deeply...

Think about those deeply in love; they may strive to impress each other, forgetting their own qualities. Despite parental objections, they may choose to be together. But what happens next?

After a few years, they may find themselves in court, seeking a divorce. Why? They realize they are not the perfect partners they once believed each other to be.

"Things are never as bad as they seem. The situations that cause us sorrow are the same ones that introduce us to the strength, power, and wisdom that we truly are."

Consider a small story: a child excitedly tells his mother about learning how to make plurals. Misunderstandings lead to a humorous situation.

Do you measure your life by the years you've lived or by your deeds within those years?

Deeds never diminish; they enrich us, revealing our importance and purpose in the eyes of the Almighty. They lead us to innovate and discover, just as the sunflower follows the sun, so should we follow our dreams.

Have you ever observed cancer or AIDS patients in a medical college? They face life with silent acceptance, having entrusted themselves to a higher power.

What are you worried about? Always about your stomach? Even at death's door, you may regret unaccomplished dreams...

See the coffin and live each day fully.

Have you ever met a contented person, satisfied with life's experiences?

There's a difference between dreams and goals: dreams require sleep, while goals demand effort.

Sometimes, we fail because we forget to try...

In the morning, look in the mirror and ask yourself if you have reasons for your actions. Be logical; are you a reasonable person?

Sometimes, the treasures of the universe come in unexpected packages. If we're too focused on what we think is best for us, we may miss what truly is.

Does that seem tasteless?

8. I Am in a Mess

"By plucking her petals, you do not gather the beauty of the flower."

- Rabindranath Tagore

Everyone seems to be trying the same approach. But why not try something different? While others throw stones at the mango tree, there's one who seeks it from a different source.

Approaching the mango tree, he stands beneath it, gazes up and prays to God. Surrounded by crows, he patiently awaits, eyes closed, unsure of what the outcome will be.

What holds you captive?

Could it be your ego?

Could it be your longing for home?

Could it be fear?

Could it be your emotions?

Life seems to balance between 50% fear and 50% fortune. Success and failure teeter on a delicate balance.

Uncertainty looms, leaving you unsure of your next move.

There are those who reside in hostels and those who long to escape to them.

There are many reasons for this. Perhaps parents are exhausted, unable to cope with their child's behavior. The child rebels, showing no respect and engaging in risky behavior.

The father's work suffers under the weight of his son's troubles. Complaints flood in from school, tarnishing the family's reputation.

The child's actions disgrace the family further. He indulges in vices, finding pleasure in rebellion.

One day, he even strikes his own mother, the woman who nurtured him. This leads to her hospitalization.

Why? She forbade him from seeing his girlfriend. Fearing his potential for violence, his parents place him in a hostel, hoping to redirect his path.

In this new environment, his routine shifts. He had to get up early. He wants to go to the mosque/temple/church to pray that he has never done in his life. He finds the life so boring. He can't even dance and have a smoke. He is totally troubled.

He called his father to pick him up. He thought about jumping many times but couldn't. Now he's facing punishment he's never faced before. He used to punish others, now he's getting punished. He can't express how much he gets hurt. He's disturbed and challenged, unable to find solace in anything.

This is just one part of his life. He stayed in the hostel, experiencing only hatred and agony. He despised his life, wanting to end it. Feeling trapped, he cut his hands with a blade.

Years passed, and now he has a routine. He wakes up early, behaves properly and has become close to many. He plans things carefully. His parents are thrilled with his progress. He respects everyone now. His family friends are amazed at his transformation. He did well in his exams. During his farewell speech, he said, "This institution and my teachers turned a criminal into someone half-decent. Why only half? Because the criminal side of me still exists. I don't know when it will resurface, but I promise to control it."

People applauded his speech, tears streaming down his face unnoticed. Despite leaving happily, he felt bored at home and wanted to return to the hostel.

Then there are students who seem perfect on the outside but are opportunistic and manipulative.

They may be nice to teachers but have ulterior motives. One such student convinced his relatives to join the same institution. Everyone praised his actions, but his letter to his brother revealed his true nature. He advised his brother to be obedient in front of authorities but play tricks behind the scenes. The principal was disappointed, realizing he had misjudged the student's character.

Now he stays in another hostel but plans to visit his old one. Who is truly great? That's for you to decide.

I recall a parable from the Bible about a father and his two sons. The father asked the first son to work in the vineyard. The son agreed but didn't go. The father asked the same to the second son, who initially refused but later changed his mind and went to work.

Who truly listened to his father? What inspired the reluctant son to change his mind?

He believes he's superior, knowing more than anyone else. He looks down on others, including his masters, seeing them as inferior to him.

If you hear people talking about such a child, one who schemes behind others' backs, what would you do? Would the person believe your words if you spoke against the candidate?

They might think you're jealous and speak ill of you. You might face criticism if you try to intervene.

You're given many opportunities to be either a victim or a creator. If you decide to paint everything in your room green, you might not get help. You need to change your perspective and vision before experimenting.

Everyone and everything has its own beauty, but not everyone sees it. If every girl thinks she looks as beautiful as Aishwarya Rai, what will be her condition? And what about boys? Would every boy need to be like Abhishek Bachchan to marry them?

True beauty comes from within. There's beauty in every creation, living or non-living. We just need to see it. Dwelling on the past while living in the present is like building a coffin without nails.

Do you still think it's tasteless?

9. Many Are Called but Few Are Chosen

"It is always wise to look ahead, but difficult to look further than you can see."

- Winston Churchill

When we handle a fish or many jasmine flowers, their scent may linger on our hands even after washing. So, find joy in giving rather than receiving.

Your actions, surroundings and circumstances shape you. Take a moment to smell your hand and discern whether it carries the aroma of fish or Jasmine.

Can you step into the same river twice? Before we embark on any repetitive journey, it touches our innermost feelings.

Imagine witnessing a child near a riverbank, slipping into the water and struggling. What would you do? Stand idly by, or rush to rescue the child? The choice is yours.

Your decision won't affect me, but consider how it touches your heart before you act.

Listen to your intuition. It's natural for most of us to rush to save a child in danger. That's just human nature; we tend to act on our instincts.

There are times when you take something very seriously. You might be leading a team, heading an institution, overseeing an entire organization or managing a company. Despite your urgency, when you call for a sudden meeting, you find your colleagues disengaged. Some are yawning or dozing off, others are distracted by their phones or other thoughts. Some even chatter about their recent purchases, oblivious to the gravity of the situation.

It's disheartening, isn't it? Who's to blame? Despite your efforts to capture their attention, they view it as a leisurely break. The important message you intended to convey becomes as inconsequential as a fallen leaf. Remember, even if you're serious, others may not share your urgency. However, your seriousness is crucial for the success of your endeavors.

When we handle various situations, we often hope for some gain or satisfaction when we succeed.

Our true commitment is reflected in our actions, showing how much we've listened to our inner voice. It's important not to get caught up in useless thoughts or let them control us.

Even if we claim to have lived a virtuous life in the past, becoming a drunkard changes how people perceive us. They judge us based on our current situation, often overlooking any improvements we've made in response to past challenges.

Sometimes, behaviors we adopt to cope with difficult times can become ingrained in our lives, overpowering us.

While some may judge us solely based on our past, it's essential to focus on the present and make decisions accordingly.

So always live a day by seeing the coffin; decide what can you do at that time.

Once, I saw one of my friends, and he came to talk to me. I noticed that his face looked sad and gloomy. I couldn't figure out what was wrong with him.

He used to be good-looking and had a strong personality. He loved reading books and knew a lot about psychology and philosophy. I know this because we studied together for a while.

He spent a lot of time with monks and had some profound experiences. They treated him like a son and shared their wisdom with him. I know this because we travelled together to learn from these monks. They were our teachers.

But something strange happened. He went to Bangalore for a job interview and aced all the tests and discussions. The interviewers were amazed by his performance. They'd never seen someone like him before.

However, during the final interview, when they asked about his expected salary and for his certificates, things took a turn. He told them he didn't have any certificates, which confused them. They asked again, and he repeated the same. They exchanged looks and asked him to wait outside.

Instead of him, they chose another candidate, leaving him disqualified. He faced similar rejections in other interviews because he lacked certificates.

Certificates seem to hold a lot of value in getting a job. Some people even go to the extent of forging them. It's ironic that someone who can write books about themselves has to fake certificates to get a job.

Then there are students who seem unaware of their own lives. They're influenced by others and end up being tools of their parents' desires. They are like frogs in a well or sacrificial animals. Their destiny seems to be decided by fate itself.

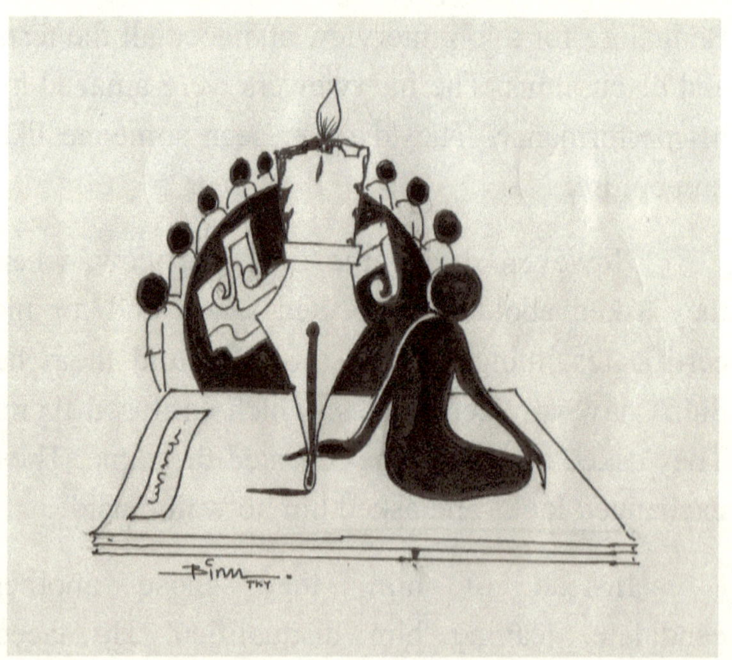

Right now, I have a simple question for you. When you visit doctors, do you often ask if they've passed their MBBS? Usually, we just get our prescriptions and go on our way. It's become a routine, almost like an experiment. But I'm sure none of us really inquire about the doctor's qualifications. Times have changed; nowadays, someone who barely passes Biology can become an MBBS doctor. How is that possible? Money seems to rule the world, guiding its course.

Imagine a father, successful in business, surrounded by friends whose children are becoming doctors and engineers. He wants to keep up, to fit in. So, he dreams of his child joining that elite group, fearing mockery otherwise. He invests heavily, sending his child to the best international schools. But truthfully, the child struggles to keep up. He's always at the bottom of the class, causing frustration for everyone. No institution wants to admit him, and wherever he goes, problems seem to follow.

Yet, the father's dream persists. He continues to push his child towards becoming a doctor, despite all the obstacles. The child faces criticism and pressure constantly. He fails every exam, surrounded by brighter students. But as the final exams approach, he throws himself into studying, day and night.

Then comes the mock exam: 2 marks in Physics, 3 marks in Biology, and a mere 1 mark in Chemistry. "Failures are the stepping stones to success," they say. In life, you may fall many times, but each time you must try to rise again. Even if you fail a thousand times, you must try one more time. You keep trying until you succeed. There will be challenges, but with perseverance, we can overcome them.

Practice and perseverance lead to excellence. Sometimes, you have to guide yourself because only you truly understand your own path.

True wisdom comes from within.

Next week is the big exam, and everyone is studying hard to prepare.

People are questioning his abilities, but no one knows why. Everyone fears failure and worries about the school's reputation. The pressure is mounting, and despite efforts, solutions seem elusive. What can be said? What can be done?

When a family friend, who was the part of the management, enquired if he had been studying, he had a witty response: "Apply, apply, but no reply."

On exam day, he woke up early, prayed briefly, and went to the other school to write the test. Despite claiming the exams were easy afterward, no one believed him given his track record.

But then came the surprise—he passed. His parents were ecstatic and threw a party to celebrate.

Eight years later, at a reunion, he shocked everyone by declaring himself a doctor, working at a prestigious hospital. Former skeptics were speechless, while some high-achieving students struggled to find jobs. Life's twists and turns are unpredictable.

He fulfilled his father's dream, but does he truly possess the skills to be a doctor? Can someone who struggled academically effectively treat patients? Perhaps his family's wealth and connections played a significant role in his success.

Yet, despite doubts about his abilities, his status remains unquestioned. It's a reminder that life is unpredictable, with opportunities often favoring the unexpected.

As the saying goes, "Many are called, but few are chosen."

Does this story feel tasteless?

10. Wake up

"The mind is not a vessel to be filled, but a fire to be kindled"

- Plutarch

Now is your moment to rise. I hope that someday each of you will achieve greatness in your lives.

Often, we get lost in dreams of a bright future, forgetting to live fully in the present. We all look ahead to tomorrow, hoping for miracles and dreaming big. Our minds soar to the highest peaks of possibility.

But remember, yesterday is past, tomorrow is unknown, and today is a precious gift. That's why it's called the present. So, embrace here and now. While you may seek to change others or your surroundings, true transformation starts within. By being a role model for change, you can influence both yourself and your environment.

Why do we feel the need to categorize people? On what grounds do we differentiate them? There's a purpose in your life, and you have a role to play in bringing about change. If you don't, who will? Do you want to leave your mark, or do you prefer to be an empty vessel?

If you believe there's a divine plan for your life, then it's up to you to fulfill it. The time to act is now. The future waits for no one.

When you make the most of today, you can create a legacy, shaping history with your actions. Have faith in yourself as the architect of your success.

"Whatever you do will be insignificant, but it is very important that you do it."

- Mahatma Gandhi

Sometimes, you might find that you only enjoy the color red. Other colors might hurt your eyes. What can you do in such a situation? Let me tell you a story:

Once, there was a man suffering from terrible eye pain. He visited many doctors, but none could figure out why. He was in great distress. Then, he met a wise man, a Saddhu, who asked him what his favorite color was. The man said it was red.

Following the Saddhu's advice, he surrounded himself with red—everything from his clothes to his surroundings. One day, his wife wore a green sari, and in a fit of anger, he threw red paint on her. This led to their divorce. See how things unfolded?

Instead of simply using a red-tinted glass, he chose to change everything around him. But here's the thing: you can't paint the world red. However, if you change your perspective, the world will appear differently. It's foolish to try and change the world without first changing yourself.

I believe that great things start with the right mindset. Our thoughts shape our words and actions, ultimately influencing our destiny.

Living in the present requires cultivating good habits. In our daily lives, we often encounter broken relationships. Have you ever wondered why? Two important aspects are learning to say "sorry" and "thank you."

Many broken relationships could be fixed if people admit their mistakes and ask for forgiveness. Honestly, we often mock Americans for apologizing too much, yet we might get upset when someone says sorry. That's how things are nowadays.

Being thankful is important. It's a way of showing appreciation and respect to others. Close friends understand this. Expressing gratitude for someone's kindness is truly valuable.

Here's a funny story to wrap up my book: Once, there was a lavish birthday party for a one-year-old in London. The parents, who seemed important, spared no expense. As expected, guests brought gifts for the baby.

One man wanted to greet the baby personally and offer a gift. He approached the well-dressed mother, who explained that she left the baby at home with the maid to avoid any disruptions to her appearance. As he glanced at the other guests, he realized why they were seated so carefully.

How do you say thank you for such a grand celebration? Birthdays have changed; sometimes, the birthday child isn't even present. Everyone is busy with their own lives, even the mother. It's sad to think the baby celebrates without experiencing his mother's love.

Do you want to follow this trend or make a change? Start today. Make your mark. Be the agent of change. The time is now.

Miracles await you. Are you living in the dawn or dusk of your life? Remember, your life has meaning.

"The hidden well – spring of your soul must need rise and run murmuring to the sea;

And the treasure of your infinite depths would be revealed to your eyes.

But let there be no scales to weigh your unknown treasure;

And seek not the depths of your knowledge with staff or sounding line."

- Kahlil Gibran, The Prophet

Epilogue

While I was asleep, I heard noises that disturbed me. I could hear my parents talking, my sister yelling at my younger brother for tracking mud inside after playing. My friends were calling out to me, disappointed after losing a cricket game we planned to watch together at 3:30 pm, but I couldn't make it.

Then, I felt something on my cheek and woke up to find my puppy sitting on my lap. I noticed my coffee had gone cold, and I glanced at the clock—it was already 6:30 pm. Checking my phone, I saw 25 missed calls from my friends. I felt bad for breaking my promise to them. They were counting on me, but I let them down.

Despite this, I thanked God for the good sleep I had and the chance to finish a book. I prayed for more peaceful nights to come, so I could read even more books.

I hope you have enjoyed living a life.

Thank you

www.ingramcontent.com/pod-product-compliance
Lightning Source LLC
Chambersburg PA
CBHW021129130726
47988CB00003B/1215